OXFORD
UNIVERSITY PRESS

Annette Succeeds in Class

Paula S. Goepfert

Illustrated by Daniel Chen

198 Madison Avenue
New York, NY 10016 USA

Great Clarendon Street, Oxford OX2 6DP UK

Oxford University Press is a department of the University of Oxford. It furthers the University's objective of excellence in research, scholarship, and education by publishing worldwide in

Oxford   New York
Auckland Cape Town Dar es Salaam
Hong Kong Karachi Kuala Lumpur Madrid
Melbourne Mexico City Nairobi New Delhi
Shanghai Taipei Toronto

With offices in
Argentina Austria Brazil Chile Czech Republic
France Greece Guatemala Hungary Italy Japan
Poland Portugal Singapore South Korea
Switzerland Thailand Turkey Ukraine Vietnam

OXFORD and OXFORD ENGLISH are registered trademarks of Oxford University Press.

Photocopying

The Publisher grants permission for the photocopying of those pages marked "photocopiable" according to the following conditions. Individual purchasers may make copies for their own use or for use by classes that they teach. School purchasers may make copies for use by staff and students, but this permission does not extend to additional schools or branches.

Under no circumstances may any part of this book be photocopied for resale.

Executive Publishing Manager: Stephanie Karras
Managing Editor: Sharon Sargent
Design Manager: Stacy Merlin
Project Coordinator: Sarah Dentry
Production Layout Artist: Colleen Ho
Cover Design: Colleen Ho, Stacy Merlin, Michael Steinhofer
Manufacturing Manager: Shanta Persaud
Manufacturing Controller: Eve Wong

ISBN: 978 0 19474035 7 (BOOK)

ISBN: 978 0 19474039 5 (OPD READING LIBRARY)

ISBN: 978 0 19474058 6 (ACADEMICS READING LIBRARY)

Printed in China

10 9 8 7 6 5 4

This book is printed on paper from certified and well-managed sources.

Many thanks to Pronk&Associates, Kelly Stern, and Meg Brooks for a job well done.

Annette Succeeds in Class

Table of Contents

A. Match the pictures with the words.

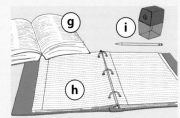

<u>e</u>   1. bookcase

___   2. bulletin board

___   3. clock

___   4. computer

___   5. dictionary

___   6. flashcard

___   7. map

___   8. notebook paper

___   9. pencil sharpener

___   10. whiteboard

B. Answer the questions.

1. Why do adults take classes?
2. What classes do you want to take? Why?
3. What makes a class easy or difficult?

C. Read the title of this book. Read the chapter titles. Look at the pictures in the book. Then guess the answers to the questions. Circle *a* or *b*.

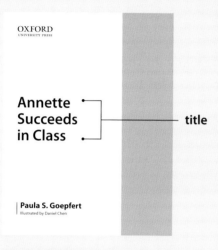

1. What is this book about?
   a. making friends
   b. doing well in a class

2. Who is Annette?
   a. a student
   b. a teacher

3. How does Annette feel about her English class?
   a. bored
   b. excited

Chapter 1

Making a Friend

Annette goes to her first English class at the Waverly Community Center. She's excited.

"My name is Ms. Wilson," the teacher says. "Look around the classroom. What do you see? Tell me the words in English."

One student raises his hand. "I see a map and a clock."

Another student says, "I see a computer."

Annette says, "I see a dictionary on the bookcase. Oh, and Ms. Wilson, do I need a dictionary for this class?"

Ms. Wilson answers, "Yes, you should all buy a dictionary." Then she says, "Now please take out your notebooks. We're going to make personal dictionaries."

Annette is embarrassed. She doesn't have a notebook.

Another student in the class sees Annette's problem. She gives Annette some notebook paper.

"My name's Ka-Ling," she says.

"Thanks!" Annette says.

Ms. Wilson writes ten words on the whiteboard. She says, "Write each word. Then write a definition or draw a picture."

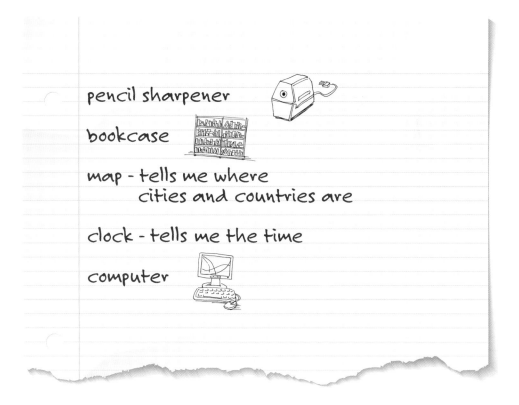

pencil sharpener

bookcase

map - tells me where
       cities and countries are

clock - tells me the time

computer

Annette starts working.

She hears Ka-Ling say, "Oh, no. I broke the point on my pencil!"

Annette sees Ka-Ling holding her pencil. Annette gives Ka-Ling her pencil sharpener.

"Thank you!" Ka-Ling says. She hands the pencil sharpener back to Annette.

Annette says, "Drawing pictures helps me with new words. Does drawing help you?"

"Yes, but I can't draw a bookcase!" laughs Ka-Ling. "Can I see your drawing?"

Annette and Ka-Ling begin working together.

After class, Annette and Ka-Ling talk outside.

Annette asks, "Why are you taking this class?"

"My son's starting school," explains Ka-Ling. "I want to help with his homework. Why are you taking the class?"

"I was a nurse in my country. I want to work as a nurse here. I need to learn more English," says Annette.

Annette's cell phone rings. She answers it and listens.

"My niece is sick," Annette says. "I have to go home."

7

A. Mark the sentences T (true) or F (false).

__T__ 1. Annette goes to her first English class.

____ 2. Annette gives some notebook paper to Ka-Ling.

____ 3. Annette is going to learn new words.

____ 4. Annette wants to work as a nurse in the United States.

____ 5. Annette's mother is sick.

B. Circle the correct word.

1. Can you find the country of Mexico on the (niece / (map))?
2. What time is it? Can you look at the (clock / homework) and tell me?
3. Please use the (nurse / computer) to type your story.
4. Please put the dictionary in the (bookcase / whiteboard).
5. I write new words on (a dictionary / notebook paper).
6. I broke my pencil point. Can I use your (pencil sharpener / notebook)?
7. I talk to my family on a (cell phone / class).

C. Work on problem solving. Match the problems and solutions.

__b__ 1. Annette needs notebook paper.

     a. Annette goes home.

____ 2. Ka-Ling breaks her pencil point.

     b. Ka-Ling gives Annette paper.

____ 3. Annette's niece is sick.

     c. Annette gives Ka-Ling a pencil sharpener.

What's going to happen next? What do you think?
Read the question. Then circle your guess, *yes* or *no*.

1. Is Annette going to work at
   the hospital?

   yes   no

2. Is Annette going to take care
   of her sick niece?

   yes   no

3. Are Annette and Ka-Ling
   going to be friends?

   yes   no

Chapter 2

Learning in Class

The next day, Annette and Ka-Ling talk before class.

"How's your niece?" asks Ka-Ling.

"She has a cold, but it's not serious," answers Annette.

Ms. Wilson arrives. She tells the class, "Today you're going to have a conversation. You're going to tell a partner about your home country."

Annette and Ka-Ling smile at each other. They want to be partners.

"You can use the map on the wall and the books in the bookcase," says Ms. Wilson.

Annette and Ka-Ling begin talking about their home countries.

"I'm from Haiti," says Annette. "Haiti is a warm country. It has beautiful mountains. People grow coffee there. In Haiti, people speak two languages, French and Creole."

"What foods do people like there?" asks Ka-Ling.

"We all like fish!" laughs Annette. "And I love mangoes."

"Where is Haiti?" asks Ka-Ling.

"Let's look at the map," says Annette.

Annette and Ka-Ling find Haiti on the map.

"What's this word?" asks Annette. She's pointing to the word *sea*.

"I don't know," says Ka-Ling. "It's in the blue part of the map. The blue part looks like an ocean."

"Let's find the meaning in the dictionary," says Annette.

The women look up *sea* in the dictionary. They learn that a sea is like a small ocean. Ka-Ling is right!

sea /si/ *noun 1* a large area of salt water. A sea is smaller than an ocean. *2* the ocean

Ka-Ling tells Annette about China, her home country.

The teacher asks, "Are you finished with your conversations?"

The students all say, "Yes."

"Now I want you to write about your home country," says Ms. Wilson. "You can use a piece of notebook paper or a computer."

Annette wants to use a computer. She doesn't know how. She feels nervous, but she asks the teacher for help.

The teacher says, "Of course I'll help you. It's easy."

A. These sentences are false. Make them true.

1. The students work alone.

   The students work with partners.

2. Haiti is a cold country.

3. The students draw a picture of their home country.

4. Annette doesn't want to use a computer.

5. Annette feels angry.

B. Cross out the item that does NOT belong in each group.

1. whiteboard	~~conversation~~	notebook paper
2. pencil	pen	partner
3. ocean	sea	island
4. fish	country	coffee
5. nervous	excited	easy

C. Work on problem solving. Circle the correct answer.

1. How do Annette and Ka-Ling find out what *sea* means?
    a. They ask the teacher.
    b. They read the word again.
    c. They look up the word in the dictionary.

2. How does Annette learn to use a computer?
    a. She asks Ka-Ling.
    b. She asks the teacher.
    c. She asks her niece for help.

What's going to happen next? What do you think?
Read the question. Then circle your guess, *yes* or *no*.

1. Is the teacher going to put the students' writing on the bulletin board?

   yes   no

2. Is Ka-Ling going to study alone?

   yes   no

3. Is Annette going to visit Haiti?

   yes   no

Chapter 3

Studying for a Test

Annette is early for class the next day. Other students are early, too. Ka-Ling is standing near the bulletin board. She calls to Annette.

"Look!" she says. "Here's our writing!"

The teacher comes into the classroom.

"Good morning!" says Ms. Wilson. "I put your work on the bulletin board. Your writing is very good. I'm proud of you. Take some time and read other people's work. You can learn new words from each other."

Soon, class begins. The students sit down at their desks.

"We're going to have a test on the new words," says the teacher. She writes *How to Study Vocabulary* on the whiteboard. She says, "Here's a good way to study new words. First, read the word and look at the picture. Second, say the word three times. Then, write the word three times. Last, cover the picture, and read the word again."

Annette and Ka-Ling study together in class. After class, Ka-Ling says, "We're good study partners!"

"We are!" says Annette. "Can we study together now?"

The women don't live near each other. They decide to stay at the community center.

"Let's work outside," says Ka-Ling.

"OK," says Annette. "We can make flashcards."

"What are flashcards?" asks Ka-Ling.

"You draw a picture on one side of the card. You write the word on the other side," says Annette.

Annette makes a flashcard. She shows the picture to Ka-Ling. "What's the word?" asks Annette.

"Pencil sharpener!" says Ka-Ling. "I see. We can use flashcards and test each other."

The women make flashcards. They test each other.

"Do you think we're ready for the test?" asks Annette.

Ka-Ling answers, "I hope so! My son can test me tonight."

Annette says, "And my niece can test me!"

"I think we're going to be ready," says Ka-Ling.

A. Choose the correct answer.

1. The teacher puts the students' writing on the ___ .
   a. bookcase
   b. computer
   c. bulletin board ✓

2. The teacher says the students are going to have a ___ .
   a. test
   b. dictionary
   c. conversation

3. After class, Annette and Ka-Ling ___ .
   a. eat their lunch
   b. study vocabulary words
   c. talk about their friends

4. Ka-Ling and Annette decide that ___ .
   a. tests are difficult
   b. they're not ready for the test
   c. their families can help them study

B. Complete the sentences. Use the words in the box.

bulletin board	early	~~flashcard~~
proud	test	

1. One side of the ___flashcard___ shows a picture.

2. I studied hard for the _____ .

3. She's _____ for class. It doesn't start until 9:00.

4. We look at the _____ to see our completed work.

5. He's very _____ of his good grade.

C. Work on problem solving. Choose the correct answer.

1. Annette and Ka-Ling don't live near each other. How do they solve this problem?

    a. They go to a mall and study.
    b. They study on the telephone.
    c. They stay at the center and study.

2. Ka-Ling doesn't know what a flashcard is. How does Annette solve this problem?

    a. She asks the teacher for help.
    b. She makes a flashcard and shows it to Ka-Ling.
    c. She decides not to use flashcards.

What's Next in Chapter 4?

What's going to happen next? What do you think?
Read the question. Then circle your guess, *yes* or *no*.

1. Is Annette going to take the test at home?

    yes   no

2. Are Annette and Ka-Ling going to meet at Ka-Ling's apartment?

    yes   no

3. Are Annette and Ka-Ling going to do well on the test?

    yes   no

Chapter 4

Taking a Test

The students are quiet. Today is the day of the test.

"The test has four parts," says Ms. Wilson. "Read the directions carefully." She writes the directions for each part on the board:

1. Fill in the blank.
2. Cross out the word.
3. Label the pictures.
4. Write 3 sentences.

"Do you have any questions?" she asks.
Annette asks, "Can we use a dictionary?"

"Yes, you can use anything in the classroom," the teacher says. "You can use the dictionary. You can use the books in the bookcase, and you can use the map. You need to work alone. You have 30 minutes to finish the test." Ms. Wilson smiles and says, "Don't be nervous. I'm sure you're all going to do well."

Annette is very nervous, but she's also excited. She's learning so much! She looks at the clock and starts the test.

The next day, all the students talk about the test. They hope the teacher is going to give them their grades.

Ms. Wilson comes into the classroom and says, "Good morning!"

The students take their seats.

"I have your tests," the teacher says. "You all did well! Everyone got an A, a B, or a C. Good work! Now I'm going to tell you what the grades mean." She draws a chart on the whiteboard.

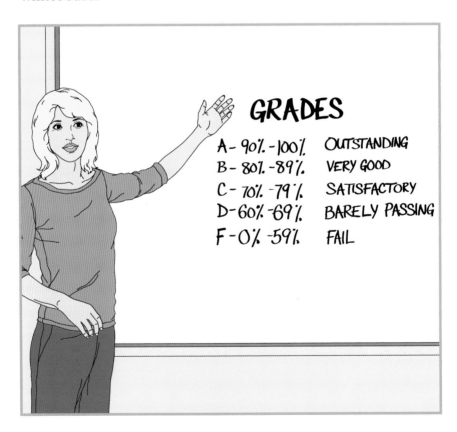

GRADES

A - 90% - 100%   OUTSTANDING
B - 80% - 89%   VERY GOOD
C - 70% - 79%   SATISFACTORY
D - 60% - 69%   BARELY PASSING
F - 0% - 59%   FAIL

Annette smiles when she sees her grade. She has an A. Ka-Ling shows Annette her test. She has an A, too!

"You can learn from your mistakes," says the teacher. "Take ten minutes and look at your test. Correct your mistakes."

Annette turns to Ka-Ling. "Do you have time for coffee after class?" she asks.

"Yes, I do! We can celebrate!" answers Ka-Ling.

Annette laughs. "We're succeeding in our class!"

Reading Check

A. Mark the sentences T (true) or F (false). Change the false sentences. Make them true.

_F_ 1. The students talk before the test.

　　　<u>The students are quiet before the test.</u>

___ 2. The test is ten minutes long.

___ 3. Annette is upset about the test.

___ 4. Annette and Ka-Ling succeed in class.

B. Complete the sentences. Use the words in the box.

celebrate	chart	grade
label	mistakes	nervous

1. A _____ gives information about a picture.

2. Most people get _____ before a test.

3. An A is an outstanding _____ on a test.

4. Fill in the _____ with these words.

5. Students can learn from their _____ .

6. People _____ when they're happy.

C. Work on problem solving. Circle the correct answer.

1. Annette thinks, "I want to use a dictionary for the test. Is that OK?"
   How does she solve this problem?
   a. She asks Ms. Wilson if it's OK.
   b. She uses a dictionary, but she doesn't ask the teacher.
   c. She doesn't use a dictionary for the test.

2. Annette feels nervous. How does she solve this problem?
   a. She leaves the classroom.
   b. She asks the teacher for more time.
   c. She thinks about how much she's learning and starts working.

What's Next?

**What's going to happen next? What do you think?
Circle your guess, *yes* or *no*.**

1. Is Annette going to learn more English?   yes   no

Today is

3. Is Ka-Ling going to be a teacher?   yes   no

2. Is Annette going to work as a nurse?   yes   no

4. Is Ka-Ling going to China?   yes   no

27

After Reading Activity

A. Read an ad for a community center.

- Read the ad to the right. What do you think you can learn in a parenting class? What do you think you can learn in a cooking class?

- Look on the Internet and in the newspaper. Find other ads like the one here. Bring the ads to class.

WHAT DO YOU WANT TO LEARN?

The Waverly Community Center offers classes in

- computers
- parenting
- cooking
- arts and crafts

and many more subjects!

When?
Monday to Friday nights, 6:30 to 8:00 p.m.

Where?
Waverly Community Center
1762 Hartson Street
512-555-2378

Why?
To learn something new!

B. Work with a partner. Write your own ad.

- Think about what your community needs. What do people need to learn?

- Write an ad for a class that teaches people new things.

- Share your ad with the class.

Useful Expressions

When is the class?

Where is the class?

What does the class offer?

Shared vocabulary from the *OPD*
and *Annette Succeeds in Class*

bookcase
[bŏŏk/ kās/]

bulletin board
[bŏŏl/ə tn börd/]

cell phone
[sĕl/ fōn/]

clock
[kläk]

coffee
[kö/fē]

computer
[kəm pyōō/tər]

dictionary
[dĭk/shə nër/ē]

fish
[fĭsh]

flashcard
[flăsh/kärd]

29

island
[ī′lənd]

A	90%-100%	Outstanding
B	80%-89%	Very good
C	70%-79%	Satisfactory
D	60%-69%	Barely passing
F	0%-59%	Fail

grades
[grādz]

mangoes
[măng′gōz]

map
[măp]

notebook paper
[nōt′bŏŏk′ pāp′ər]

nurse
[nürs]

pencil sharpener
[pĕn′səl shär′pə nər]

test
[tĕst]

whiteboard
[wīt′börd′]